700
TI

D0116849

SOME FLOWERS

VITA SACKVILLE-WEST

SOME FLOWERS

WATERCOLORS BY
GRAHAM RUST

HARRY N. ABRAMS, INC.
PUBLISHERS

DESIGNED BY DAVID FORDHAM

LIBRARY OF CONGRESS CATALOGING-IN-PUBLICATION DATA

SACKVILLE-WEST, V. (VICTORIA), 1892–1962.
    SOME FLOWERS / VITA SACKVILLE-WEST; WATERCOLORS BY GRAHAM RUST.
        P.   CM.
    ORIGINALLY PUBLISHED: LONDON: COBDEN-SANDERSON, 1937,
    ISBN 0–8109–3837–5
    1. FLOWERS.   2. FLOWER GARDENING.   I. RUST, GRAHAM.   II. TITLE.
SB407.S265 1993
635.9——DC20   93–12281

TEXT COPYRIGHT © 1937 VITA SACKVILLE-WEST
ILLUSTRATIONS COPYRIGHT © 1993 GRAHAM RUST

PUBLISHED IN 1993 BY HARRY N. ABRAMS, INCORPORATED, NEW YORK
A TIMES MIRROR COMPANY
ALL RIGHTS RESERVED. NO PART OF THE CONTENTS OF THIS BOOK MAY BE
REPRODUCED WITHOUT THE WRITTEN PERMISSION OF THE PUBLISHER

FIRST PUBLISHED IN 1993 BY PAVILION BOOKS LIMITED, LONDON

PRINTED AND BOUND IN ITALY

PLATES AND COMMENTARIES

PREFACE

 N 1937, VICTORIA SACKVILLE-WEST, THE aristocratic wife of Harold Nicolson, Member of Parliament and former diplomat, published *Some Flowers,* a slim volume about her favourite flowers.

What might sound like a somewhat dilettante production was in fact nothing of the kind. At the time she was a well-known poet and novelist. She was also an expert gardener, busy turning the garden of Sissinghurst Castle into the most famous and influential in England.

Vita Sackville-West was born in 1892 at Knole, in Kent, the family seat granted by Elizabeth 1 to Thomas Sackville and the largest privately owned property in England. There she grew up, an only child, with her parents and Lord Sackville, her grandfather. A snobbish and domineering child, as she later admitted, she had few friends and lived to a large extent in a world of her own. She loved the vast, rambling house, filled with family portraits, and the Kentish countryside, and from them developed a profound love of history and a deeply engrained sense of place which never left her.

Knole was her first great love – she would write later of the 'umbilical cord' connecting her to it – and her greatest loss. Her grandfather died when she was seventeen, and although, in a much publicized court case, her father and mother, his nephew and illegitimate daughter respectively, successfully defended their right to the house and the title, the victory was overshadowed for Vita by the realization that the house would eventually pass through the male line to her uncle and then her cousin, not to her.

Although the sense of loss was to remain with Vita throughout her life, hers was a romantic nature and she turned down more than one proposal of marriage which would have made her the mistress of another great house, choosing instead to marry for love. Harold Nicolson, whom she first met in 1910, was a brilliant young diplomat with a passion for literature and travel that matched her own. They were married in 1913, and following their return from a diplomatic posting to Constantinople their first son, Ben, was born at Knole as war began.

In 1915 Harold and Vita bought Long Barn, a substantial 'cottage' near Knole, which they extended by grafting on to it an ancient barn. With help from architect Sir Edwin Lutyens, Harold planned the design of the garden, in which his firm lines and features were complemented by Vita's instinctive flair for planting. The influences of Knole, Italy and gardener Gertrude Jekyll filtered through her romantic temperament to produce an effusive, luxuriant and natural style of gardening which would find its ultimate expression at Sissinghurst.

It was in 1918, a year after the birth of their second son, Nigel, that the marriage was threatened by Vita's discovery of her true sexuality. She had already had a lesbian affair with a childhood friend, but the sudden flowering of her love for Violet Trefusis (née Keppel) into a passionate romance was a *coup de foudre*. The story of their affair, the elopement to France and their pursuit and retrieval by their husbands has been sensitively recounted by Nigel

Nicolson in his *Portrait of a Marriage*. Out of this turbulence came calm and stability. Vita would have other lovers, including Virginia Woolf, who modelled her *Orlando* on Vita, but none thereafter to put at risk their marriage and creative partnership. Harold had already admitted to her his own homosexuality, and instead of being a double setback to the marriage, their parallel natures proved to be its salvation. Recognizing that they mattered more to each other than any other attachments, however urgent at the time, each received from the other complete freedom, honesty and trust.

In Sissinghurst Castle, the Elizabethan ruin which they bought in 1930, they found the project that would occupy the rest of their life together. They restored the surviving buildings and set to work on the wilderness which was to become, over the next three decades, one of the most perfect and individual gardens to be found anywhere. It was conceived from the first as a harmonious sequence of small, enclosed areas – the cottage garden, the rose garden, the herb garden, the nuttery – with the contrast of the large, peaceful orchard, enclosed by the moat. The white garden would be added after the war. Each garden was to have its own character, but the sheer profusion of the planting, colours arranged with infinite care and total naturalness, old roses mingling everywhere and climbers cascading over walls, gave it a uniquely personal and cohesive sense of spontaneity and romance.

Some Flowers, published in 1937, receives only a couple of lines in Victoria Glendinning's definitive biography of Vita, and, even more surprisingly, only a passing reference in *Vita's Other World*, the otherwise admirable and very thorough 'gardening biography' by Jane Brown. Yet, in its modest way, this collection of flower 'portraits' may be seen in retrospect as a landmark in Vita's life.

By now the garden was well established, and in the following year was opened to the public for the first time, on a weekend in June. In 1938 Vita also began writing gardening articles for the *New Statesman* and other magazines. These appeared in book form

the same year as *Country Notes*. After the war she began a weekly
column in the *Observer* which lasted for fifteen years and won her a
huge following. In 1951 she published *In Your Garden*, a collection
of her *Observer* writings which included most of the pieces in *Some
Flowers*. Three more such collections followed, and in 1968, six
years after her death, a selection from these four books appeared
as *Vita Sackville-West's Garden Book*.

In *Some Flowers* she hit her stride as a gardening writer at the
first attempt. With apparently effortless precision she provides
brilliantly expressive pen portraits of twenty-five favourite flowers
– their appearance, characteristics and preferred growing conditions. It is a practical book, full of expertise and sound advice, as
well as a literary *tour de force*, and it is all done in the relaxed, con-
versational tone of one gardening enthusiast addressing another
which made her journalism so approachable and popular.

She defines the flowers she chose to include as those which are
individually lovely in shape, colouring, marking or texture, 'flowers
which painters have delighted, or should delight, to paint'. It must
have been frustrating only to be able to illustrate them with black-
and-white photographs which failed to do justice to their subtle
beauty or 'answer' her words. Indeed she referred several times in
her text to the shortcomings of the photographs – and these are
the sole remarks in the original book to have been omitted from
this new edition, where happily they would have been redundant.
For in Graham Rust the publisher has found the ideal illustrator
for Vita's work. Rust specializes in murals and botanical water-
colours, twin preoccupations with large effects and exquisite detail
which would have struck a chord with her. His charming depic-
tions of the flowers echo her words with remarkable clarity,
emphasizing the accuracy and ingenuity of her descriptions. They
would surely have gladdened her heart.

FOREWORD

HIS SHORT BOOK IS VERY PERSONAL AND therefore very arbitrary. It represents nothing more than a couple of dozen among the plants I like to grow in my own garden and at first sight it may seem that there are no connecting links in this choice of plants at all. I hope I can explain that there are. The book is addressed not to the professional but to the amateur gardener. This country is a country of garden-lovers, and it contains many who, getting perhaps a little bored with growing exactly the same things as their neighbours year after year, look round for a few extras which shall come well within the scope of their purse, time, and knowledge. We can all grow our wallflowers, lupins, delphiniums or snapdragons. Far be it from me to run down any of these valuable allies, but the moment always comes when the taste of every true flower-lover turns also towards something less usual and obvious. It is this type of gardener that I have in mind. Although each of the flowers I have chosen to describe is comparatively easy to grow and inexpensive to buy, it has I think a quality of its own and is also something which is not always to be seen in every garden.

By this quality of its own, I mean something which deserves to be called 'a painter's flower'. That is to say, its beauty, neither garish nor effective at first sight, requires to be looked into and esteemed by a standard of values quite different from those by which we judge, say, an herbaceous border by the mass of colour it presents at the height of summer. The flowers I have chosen for this small book have nothing to do with the big garden proper, although they may (some of them) find a place in it. The flowers I have chosen depend chiefly on their loveliness of shape, colouring, marking, or texture. On the whole, they are flowers which require to be looked at very intimately, if their queerness or beauty is to be closely appreciated. They are flowers which painters have delighted, or should delight, to paint.

II

It is very difficult to write about flowers. I discovered this truth only when I started to do so. Before I tried my hand at it myself, I had done nothing but rail against those who were trying to do the same thing. I found myself losing my temper frequently with the nauseating sentimental phraseology which seems to impose itself on all those otherwise sincere and honest gardeners who feel impelled to transmit their knowledge and experience and emotions to other and more ignorant people. It seemed to me that they all employed the same sickly vocabulary, which deserved a dictionary to itself, so inevitable and recurrent were the terms they used.

It is very difficult indeed to write about flowers.

Think – if we are to come down to details – how difficult it is even to express in ordinary language so simple a fact as that a flower smells good. There is no other possible term in plain in English by which we may describe this attribute. If we say 'it smells', we automatically imply that it smells bad. So, instead of the honest word 'smell', are we to be forced to the genteel substitutions 'scent' or 'perfume', – neither of which conveys in the least what we mean when we say a flower smells good? 'Smells good' is an honest phrase at least, and neither 'scent' nor 'perfume' nor 'odour' or 'fragrance' can take its place. They must all be relegated to the special dictionary of writers on flowers and gardens, in which 'quaint', 'dainty', and 'winsome' must also take dishonourable rank.

Colour offers another trap. Not only is colour almost impossible to render vividly in words but unless you are to go on repeating the word over and over again, you are reduced to such evasions as 'hue' and 'colourful', – the latter an Americanism which I refuse to adopt. 'Hue' I think is just permissible when very specially and nicely applied; otherwise inexcusable. Farrer stands out among botanical writers who have managed to suggest something of the colour-quality of flowers; and *he* has been accused of being too poetical and rhetorical. He was, admittedly, a conscious stylist. Still, his descriptions must rank high, both as regards lyrical prose and botanical precision. Take, for example, his account of the first time he ever beheld the gentian which bears his name – it is only one passage amongst many which might be quoted:

> 'And its beauty! Nothing could I foretell of its temper and future history that day, as I stood rapt in contemplation before the actual plant . . . A fine frail tuft like grass radiating some half a dozen fine flapping stems – that is G. Farreri, quite inconspicuous and obscure in all the high lawns of the Da-Tung . . . Until it flowers; and every day in early September brings a fresh crashing explosion of colour in the fold of the lawns. For each of those weakly stems concludes in one enormous upturned trumpet, more gorgeous than anything attained by G. Gentianella, but in the same general style and form. But the outline is different with a

more subtle swell to the chalice, and that is freaked outside
in heavy lines of purple-black that divide long vandykes of
dim periwinkle blue with panels of Nankeen buff between:
inside the tube and throat are white, but the mouth and the
wide gold flanges are of so luminous and intense a light
azure that one blossom of it will blaze out at you among the
grass on the other side of the valley. In no other plant,
except perhaps, Ipomoea Learii, or Nemophila, do I know
such a shattering acuteness of colour: it is like a clear sky
soon after sunrise, shrill and translucent, as if it had a light
inside. It literally burns in the alpine turf like an electric
jewel, an incandescent turquoise.'

Now you may like that kind of writing or you may not:
personally I find in it an extravagance and *bravura* which please me,
and which convey to me something of the excitement and enthusi-
asm which fired the author. They please me all the more, that in
spite of the excitement he never loses sight of his standards of
comparison: 'in no other plant, except perhaps, Ipomea Learii, or
Nemophila. . . '. He can be accurate as well as extravagant.

Then there is D. H. Lawrence. One does not think of Lawrence
primarily as a writer on flowers, yet no one was more sensitively
alive to their beauty than he or more capable of reproducing it in
words. The contrast between his writing and Farrer's is instructive:
Farrer, half poet, half botanist; Lawrence, wholly poet. Here he is
speaking of the red anemone, which characteristically he prefers to
call the 'Adonis-blood anemone', whereas Farrer in spite of all his
lyricism would have called it 'Anemone fulgens':

'If you are passing in the sun, a sudden scarlet faces on to
the air, one of the loveliest scarlet apparitions in the world.
The inner surface of the Adonis-blood anemone is as fine as
velvet, and yet there is no suggestion of pile, not as much as
on a velvet rose. And from this inner smoothness issues the

red colour, perfectly pure and unknown of earth, no earthi-
ness, and yet solid, not transparent. How a colour manages
to be perfectly strong and impervious, yet of a purity that
suggests condensed light, yet not luminous, at least, not
transparent, is a problem. The poppy in her radiance is
translucent, and the tulip in her utter redness has a touch of
opaque earth. But the Adonis-blood anemone is neither
translucent nor opaque. It is just pure condensed red, of a
velvetiness without velvet, and a scarlet without glow.'

There is one thing, however, which both Farrer and Lawrence have
in common in spite of their differences: they both write with
violence and not with sentimentality. To them both, a flower is a
vibrating, living thing, endowed with qualities which are far
beyond the reach of mere botany. To Farrer, his gentian burns 'as
if it had a light inside'. To Lawrence, the anemone 'issues the red
colour, perfectly pure and unknown of earth'. They both, in
short, approach the flower as though it were a mystical thing,
reflecting on each some strange beauty which is to be found
in perfection only in another, unknown world. But neither of
them attempts to sentimentalise. They are both moving on quite
another and a higher plane.

III

All this has led me away from my own book and the difficulties
which rose up against me. These difficulties, I found, increased
because in a very short space I had to combine the descriptive
with the practical – petals, in fact, with slugs; loveliness with
manure; lavishness, with instructions for pruning. Successful
gardening is made up of all these things, and to be a successful
gardener one must also be a realist. But if one tries to compress it
all into two pages, the two manners must necessarily clash. I have

thus tried to give some idea of what a plant looks like, and also of the way it likes to be treated and of the dangers it especially dislikes to face. This was neither an easy nor a satisfactory experiment to attempt.

I ought to add another word in explanation. If sometimes I have recommended growing plants in pots or pans rather than in the open ground, this is not because any of my choice is 'difficult', but merely because a small flower is apt to get lost in the open, disappearing among the jungle of its coarser neighbours, or getting so splashed by the rain and mud that half its beauty is gone. To get the full enjoyment out of it, it should be isolated, its face should be clean and its leaves also. For this reason I have sometimes also recommended cutting the flowers and bringing them indoors. My flowers are mostly (not all) intimate flowers, which gain from being intimately observed; and this can only be done when one can pick up the pot or vase off a table, and stare in odd moments when one has nothing else to do.

SOME FLOWERS

THE
COMMENTARIES

HAMMAMELIS MOLLIS
WITCH HAZEL

AMMAMELIS MOLLIS IS PERHAPS MORE familiar to many people when they meet it in a bottle under the name Witch Hazel or Hazeline, but to the gardener it means a small shrubby tree, covered in the early part of the year with curly spider-like flowers on its naked branches. There is a particular charm about all trees which carry their flowers before their leaves, such as the almond or the judas: they have a cleanness of design, undisturbed by tufts of green; they allow us to observe the fine tracery of the twigs, while at the same time offering us some colour to look at. The Witch Hazel is certainly a tree which every one should grow, for its merits are many, and if it has a fault I have yet to discover it.

Mollis, from China, is the best of the family, which includes also two from America (Virginiana and vernalis) and one from Japan (Japonica). It is perfectly hardy and even the flowers do not wilt in a heavy frost. It likes a sunny place, where it has room to develop and although it will not revenge itself upon you by perishing outright in a poor soil but will struggle vehemently even against the stickiest clay, it will also show its gratitude for a good

loam with some leaf-mould mixed in. Another of its virtues is that it starts flowering at a very tender age, so that there is none of that long weary wait of years until the plant has reached a certain size before embarking on the business which made us desire it. From the very first it is possible to pick it for indoors, and there are few things more welcome at the churlish time of the year when it occurs. New Year's Day may see it open; perhaps even Christmas Day. The queer, wriggly, yellow petals with the wine-stained calyx at their base will last for quite ten days in water, especially if you bring it indoors while still just in the bud, and will smell far more delicious than you would believe possible if you had only sniffed it out in the cold winter air. So delicious is it, that the owner of one small new tree begins to long for the day when he can cut big generous branches instead of the few twigs which is all that he can get at first. Every one of these twigs, however, will be doing its best, and flowering on all its little length.

The leaves come later, at the ordinary time for leaves, and you can forget comfortably about your Witch Hazel during all the months when so many other things give you flowers for your garden and your vase. You need remember it again only when your supply has failed and in despair you go out to look for something to keep you company indoors. And there they will be, those curly yellow petals, ready once more to scent the room and put brightness on the table.

Iris Unguicularis

commonly but inaccurately called

STYLOSA

HIS PALE AND LOVELY ALGERIAN SHOULD fill a neglected corner in every garden. I say neglected, because no one could pretend that the untidy clumps of long straggling leaves are objects that anyone wants to look at more than necessary. It is a plant one grows for the sake of cutting its flowers, and a lavish reward will be yours during the grimmest months of the year if you only give it the treatment it enjoys.

Luckily this treatment is so simple as to amount to ill-treatment. Frail and delicate in appearance, the Algerian is really a tough which flourishes best in a sort of rubbish heap of its own. If you plant it in rich soil, and allow it so much as to catch sight of a lump of manure, its crop of leaves will be indeed extravagant, but blossoms there will be none. But if you plant it in contemptible rubbish such as brick-bats and gravel, with the especial addition of any old mortar rubble which the builders may have left over, and which is rich in lime, you will get a crop of flowers from January to March to fill every glass you may have available. The supply of lime is important, but otherwise starvation is practically all that this iris asks of you. The best I have ever seen were

growing in these conditions: one lot was growing in a gravel path with a bed of ashes under the path, and that was in England: the other lot was in Italy, on the very edge of a rough-walled terrace. I picked, and as I picked I noticed the extreme dryness and drainage thus naturally provided: there was really no soil at all in which it could indulge its mischievous habit of luxuriating if given the chance.

The foot of a warm south wall suits it best in this sun-starved country. Remember that it needs all the sun it can get: so avoid growing tall plants in front of it, and even cut back its own leaves in May or early June to allow the ripening sun to reach the heart of the clump. If your warm south wall also happens to be the wall of a greenhouse with hot-water pipes running inside, you will probably be able to start picking before Christmas. And if you want to move it from one position to another, do so for choice in September, but in any case take it up in large lumps, for it hates being disturbed. Take it up so that it doesn't notice; don't pull it to pieces with the idea of making four plantings out of one. If you treat it in this miserly fashion, it will take its revenge on you by not giving you a single bloom for at least two years.

The flower which rises surprisingly from the welter of its untidy leaves is lavender in colour and fragile in texture. The odd fact that it happens in mid-winter makes us think it far more curious than it really is. The flower, when you come to look into it, is not really subtle at all: it is not a flower which would gain anything from being put under the magnifying glass. Still, one loves it for its rathe delicacy; it is amusing to pick such fragile things springing out of the snow, one loves it, but unfortunately the slugs and snails love it too. There is nothing like the closely-folded bud of Iris unguicularis to tempt the slug and snail from their winter retreats. So put down your traps in good time, whether they are orange-peel placed upside down or little heaps of bran and powdered Meta (perhaps the best trap of all, since it

kills as well as entices), and pick your beds every day. You need have no hesitation in picking a bud even if it is still as tightly rolled as a new umbrella. Bring it into a warm room, and you can actually watch the petals unfold as it stands glassed upon your table. It is not often that one can enjoy such a pleasure, except in those quick-motion films of nasturtiums growing or wild-flowers struggling up towards existence under a hedge.

Iris Reticulata

HEN FLOWERS COME SO THICK IN SUMMER that one hesitates which to pick among so many, one is apt to forget the bare cold days when the earth is a miser offering only one or two, take it or leave it. Wrapped in mufflers and overcoats we go and peer about for a stray sprig of winter-sweet, a splashed and muddy hellebore, a premature violet – anything, anything to fill one solitary glass with some pretence of spring long before spring has really arrived. There are the bulbs, of course, which one has carefully plunged in ashes or placed in a dark cupboard, according to the instructions in the garden books and catalogues: but somehow there is always something a little artificial about any flower which has been compelled to bloom before its time. Even though we may not number ourselves among the rich who languidly fill their rooms on an order to the florist with lilac at Christmas and tulips on New Year's Day, there is still, I think, a great difference between the flowers which we force and those which we have the patience to wait for at their proper season. For one thing, the forced flower always slightly spoils our delight in its outdoor successor when it normally arrives; and for another, the

forced flower itself, however welcome, is always something of a fake. To the true lover of flowers, these arguments are disturbingly potent.

The moral of all this is, that we especially welcome any flower which lightens the gloom of winter of its own accord. The more fragile and improbable-looking, the better. Such a flower is Iris reticulata. It seems extraordinary that anything so gay, delicate, and brilliant should really prefer the rigours of winter to the amenities of spring. It is true that we can grow Iris reticulata in pots under glass if we wish to do so, and that the result will be extremely satisfying and pretty, but the far more pleasing virtue of Iris reticulata is that it will come into bloom out of doors as early as February, with no coddling or forcing at all. Purple flecked with gold, it will open its buds even above the snow. The ideal place to grow it is in a pocket of rather rich though well-drained soil amongst stones; a private place which it can have all to itself for the short but grateful days of its consummation.

Iris reticulata – the netted iris. Not the flower is netted, but the bulb. The bulb wears a little fibrous coat, like a miniature fishing-net. It is a native of the Caucasus, and there is a curious fact about it: the Caucasian native is reddish, whereas our European garden form is a true Imperial purple. Botanists, including Mr W. R. Dykes, the greatest authority on irises, have been puzzled by the Mendelian characteristics exhibited by this group. Mr Dykes received bulbs from the Caucasus, which were always reddish, the garden form was purple, and yet the seedlings he raised from the garden form were always reddish again. It was only in the fourth generation, raised from seed, that he re-obtained the purple form, and even that differed slightly in colour from the fixed garden type.

It is unlikely that any of us will wish to experiment with our own saved seeds in this way, but still I throw it out as a suggestion to those who have the inclination and the leisure. (Let me warn

those enthusiasts that they will have to wait for at least four years between the sowing of the seed and the flowering of the bulb.) In the meantime I do suggest that every flower-lover should grow a patch of the little reticulata somewhere in his garden. Let me also draw his attention to the variety known as I. reticulata Cantab, rather expensive at present (about 1s. a bulb) which is as bright a blue as Gentiana verna. This, however, being an expensive treasure, is better grown in a pot under glass. It would be a pity to buy it and then lose it.

FRITILLARIA IMPERIALIS
THE CROWN IMPERIAL

IKE THE OTHER MEMBERS OF ITS FAMILY, the stateliest of them all has the habit of hanging its head, so that you have to turn it up towards you before you can see into it at all. Then and then only will you be able to observe the delicate veining on the pointed petals. It is worth looking into these yellow depths for the sake of the veining alone, especially if you hold it up against the light, when it is revealed in a complete system of veins and capillaries. You will, however, have to pull the petals right back, turning the secretive bell into something like a starry dahlia, before you can see the six little cups, so neatly filled to the brim, not overflowing, with rather watery honey at the base of each petal, against their background of dull purple and bright green. Luckily it does not seem to resent this treatment at all and allows itself to be closed up again into the bell-like shape which is natural to it, with the creamy pollened clapper of its stamens handing down the middle.

Perhaps some people may hold me wrong for including the Crown Imperial among my so-called 'painter's flowers'. The reason I thus include it, is that it always reminds me of the stiff,

Gothic-looking flowers one sometimes sees growing along the bottom of a mediaeval tapestry, together with irises and lilies in a fine disregard for season. Grown in a long narrow border, especially at the foot of an old wall of brick or stone, they curiously reproduce this effect. It is worth noting also how well the orange of the flower marries with really rosy brick, far better than any of the pink shades which one might more naturally incline to put against it. It is worth noting also that you had better handle the bulbs in gloves for they smell stronger than garlic.

It was once my good fortune to come unexpectedly across the Crown Imperial in its native home. A dark, damp ravine in one of the wildest parts of Persia, a river rushed among boulders at the bottom, the overhanging trees turned the greenery almost black, ferns sprouted from every crevice of the mossy rocks, water dripped everywhere, and in the midst of this moist lavishness I suddenly discerned a group of the noble flowers. Its coronet of orange bells glowed like lanterns in the shadows in the mysterious place. The narrow track led me downwards towards the river, so that presently the banks were towering above me, and now the Crown Imperials stood up like torches between the wet rocks, as they had stood April after April in wasteful solitude beside that

unfrequented path. The merest chance that I had lost my way had brought me into their retreat; otherwise I should never have surprised them thus. How noble they looked! How well-deserving of their name! Crown Imperial — they did indeed suggest an orange diadem fit to set on the brows of the ruler of an empire.

That was a strange experience, and one which I shall never forget. Since then, I have grown Crown Imperials in my own garden. They are very handsome, very sturdy, very Gothic. But somehow that Persian ravine has spoiled me for the more sophisticated interpretation which I used to associate with the Crown Imperial. Somehow I can no longer think of them solely as the flowers one sees growing along the bottom of a mediaeval tapestry. I think of them as the imperial wildings I found by chance in a dark ravine in their native hills.

Fritillaria Meleagris
The Meadow Fritillary

 UR NATIVE FRITILLARY IS ONE OF THOSE strange flowers which does not seem indigenous to our innocent pastures at all. There are some such flowers – the wild arum, for instance, and many of the orchises, whom nobody would take for anything but exotics. The fritillary looks like something exceedingly choice and delicate and expensive, which ought to spring from a pan in a hot-house, rather than share the fresh grass with buttercups and cowslips. Its very nick-names have something sinister about them: Snakeshead, the Sullen Lady, and sometimes The Leper's Bell. Yet it is as much of a native as the blue-bell or the ragged robin.

Some people mistake it for a kind of wild tulip, others for a daffodil; Gilbert White of Selborne is one of those who fell into the latter error. Miss Mitford does even worse, in calling it 'the tinted wood anemone'. It belongs in fact to the *liliaceae* and so might accurately be called our own private English lily of the fields. Its curious square markings explain several of its various names: *fritillus*, for instance, is the Latin for dice-box, which in its turn had been named from a chess or chequer-board; and *meleagris*

derives from the Latin for the guinea-fowl, whose speckled feathers so vividly reminded our ancestors of the fritillary that Gerard in his *Herbal* (1597) frankly calls it the Ginny-Hen flower.

It is unfortunately becoming rarer every year, and is extremely local in its distribution. That is to say, where you find it at all, you find it generously by the acre, and where you do not find it you simply have to go without. Unlike the orchises, there is no chance of coming across a few here and there although the supply may not be lavish: the fritillary knows no half measures. When you have once seen it by the acre, however, it is a sight not likely to be forgotten. Less showy than the buttercup, less spectacular than the foxglove, it seems to put a damask shadow over the grass, as though dusk were falling under a thunder-cloud that veiled the setting sun. For when it grows at all, it can grow as thick as the blue-bell, sombre and fuscous, singularly unsuitable to the water-meadows and the willows of an Oxfordshire or a Hampshire stream. In wine-making countries one has seen the musty heaps of crushed discarded grape-skins after the juice has been pressed from them. Their colour is then almost exactly that of the meadow fritillary.

In its native state the bulb grows very deep down, so taking a hint from nature we ought to plant it in our own gardens at a depth of at least six to eight inches. There is another good reason for doing this: pheasants are fond of it, and are liable to scratch it up if planted too shallow. Apart from its troubles with pheasants, it is an extremely obliging bulb and will flourish almost anywhere in good ordinary soil, either in grass or in beds. It looks best in grass, of course, where it is naturally meant to be, but I do not think it much matters where you put it, since you are unlikely to plant the million bulbs which would be necessary in order to reproduce anything like the natural effect, and are much more likely to plant just the few which will give you enough flowers for picking. For the fritillary, unless you are prepared to grow it on

the enormous scale to which it naturally inclines, is a flower to put in a glass on your table. It is a flower to peer into. In order to appreciate its true beauty, you will have to learn to know it intimately. You must look closely at all its little squares, and also turn its bell up towards you so that you can look right down into its depths, and see the queer semi-transparency of the strangely foreign, wine-coloured chalice. It is a sinister little flower, sinister in its mournful colours of decay.

TULIPA CLUSIANA
THE LADY TULIP

HE IS FAMILIARLY CALLED THE LADY TULIP, but actually reminds one most of a regiment of little red and white soldiers. Seen growing wild on Mediterranean or Italian slopes, you can imagine a Liliputian army deployed at its spring manœuvres. I suppose her alleged femineity is due to her elegance and neatness, with her little white shirt so simply tucked inside her striped jacket, but she is really more like a slender boy, a slim little officer dressed in a parti-coloured uniform of the Renaissance.

Clusiana is said to have travelled from the Mediterranean to England in 1636, which, as the first tulips had reached our shores about 1580, is an early date in tulip history. Unlike Lars Porsena, she has nothing to do with Clusium, but takes her name from Carolus Clusius (or Charles de Lecluse) who became Professor of botany at Leiden in 1593. Her native home will suggest the conditions under which she likes to be grown: a sunny exposure and a light rich soil. If it is a bit gritty, so much the better. Personally I like to see her springing up amongst grey stones, with a few rather stunted shrubs of Mediterranean character to keep

her company: some dwarf lavender, and the grey-green cistus making a kind of amphitheatre behind her while some creeping rosemary spreads a green mat at her feet. The rosemary should normally be in flower at the same time as the tulip, *i.e.* towards the second half of April, and a few neighbouring clumps of the blue Anemone Apennina would associate perfectly both as to colour and to quality with the small pale bluish-lilac flowers of the rosemary. A grouping of this kind has the practical advantage that all its members enjoy the same treatment as to soil and aspect, and, being regional compatriots, have the air of understanding one another and speaking the same language. Nothing has forced them into an ill-assorted companionship.

If the extent and disposition of one's garden allows one to indulge in such luxuries as these little pockets of 'regional gardening,' how lucky one is! Half the secret of planting lies in happy association. Some plants 'go' together; others, most definitely, do not. There can be no rule, for it is essentially a question of taste and flair, but if a rule can be made at all it is that nature's own arrangements are usually the best. One has only to think of the innumerable tiny alpine gardens lavished all over the high pastures of the mountains, to see how perfectly and effortlessly the job is done. A solitary huge boulder, a cushion of silence pressed against it, a few mauve violas blowing lightly a foot away, a dab of pink thrift, some blue lances of Gentiana verna, and there it is, complete. No overcrowding, no anomalies. Just three or four square yards of minute perfection round which you could put a frame, detaching them from the sunny immensity and leaving them just as self-contained, self-sufficient. . . .

In this way one may steal sections out of one's own garden and make self-contained satisfactory small enclosures, such as the scrap of Mediterranean hillside, in which to grow the scrubby lavender, the bushy cistus, the creeping rosemary, the blue anemone, and the slim little Lady Tulip who is more like a boy.

PRIMULA AURICULA

URICULAS ARE OF TWO KINDS, ONE FOR THE rich man and one for the poor. There is no denying that the kind known as the Show auriculas, which demands to be grown under glass, is the more varied and exquisite in its colourings and markings and general strangeness. Above the mealy stems and leaves, looking as though they had been dusted with powdered chalk, rise the flat heads, curiously scalloped with a margin of contrary colour, it may be of white or gold or green, or of purple or a reddish bronze, all as velvet as a pansy:

> Their gold, their purples, scarlets, crimson dyes,
> Their dark and lighter-haired diversities,
> With all their pretty shades and ornaments,
> Their parti-coloured coats and pleasing scents. . . .
> In double ruffs, with gold and silver laced,
> On purpose crimson, and so neatly placed.

So greatly did the old florists esteem the Show auricula, that they used to stage it in miniature theatres, something like Punch

and Judy, painting pictures in the interior of the theatre in order to give interest to their gardens when the plants were not in flower.

But although we may have modestly to content ourselves with the outdoor or Alpine Auricula, we have nothing to complain of, for it is not only the painter's but also the cottagers' flower. It is indeed one of those flowers which looks more like the invention of a miniaturist or of a designer of embroidery, than like a thing which will grow easily and contentedly in one's own garden. But in practical truth it will flourish gratefully given the few conditions it requires: a deep, cool root-run, a light soil with plenty of leaf-mould (some of the old growers recommended the soil thrown up from mole-hills), a certain amount of shade during the hotter hours of the day, and enough moisture to keep it going. In other words, a west or even a north aspect will suit it well, so long as you do not forget the deep root-run, which has the particular reason that the auricula roots itself deeper and deeper into the earth as it grows older. If you plant it in shallow soil, you will find that the plant hoists itself upwards, away from the ground, eventually raising itself on to a bare, unhappy-looking stem, whereas it really ought to be flattening its leaves against the brown earth, and making rosette after rosette of healthy green. If your auriculas are doing this, you may be sure they are doing well, and you may without hesitation dig them up and divide them as soon as they have ceased flowering, that is to say in May or June, and re-plant the bits you have broken off, to increase your group next year.

It is well worth trying to raise seedlings from your own seed, for you never know what variation you may get. The seed germinates easily in about ten days or a fortnight; sow it in a sandy compost, barely covering the seed; keep the seedlings in a shady place, in pots if you like, or pricked out on a suitable border till they are big enough to move to their permanent home. At one time, auricula seed was worth ten guineas an ounce, so perhaps

this reflection ought to inspire us with some reverence for the quantity which nature supplies gratis.

Auriculas have a long history behind them. It is suggested that they may have been known to the Romans, as a plant whose native home was the Alps. With more certainty we know that they derive their name from the supposed resemblance of their leaves to the ears of bears: *Oreille d'ours* in French, *Orecchia d'orso* in Italian; a somewhat far-fetched resemblance, I think, but one which obtained general credence. Huguenot refugees popularised them in England, and by the latter half of the seventeenth century many new varieties had been raised, to which some charming and fanciful names were given, such as the Fair Virgin, the Alderman, the Matron, Prince Silverwings, and a white novelty called the Virgin's Milk. The most pleasing and descriptive of all names, however, is the old Dusty Miller, more pleasing even than the name Vanner's aprons, as they were called in Gloucestershire, no doubt in allusion to the tough leathery texture of the leaves. They appear also to have been called Baziers, but Baziers is a word I cannot trace, even in the big Oxford English Dictionary. I wonder if it can possibly have any reference to aprons made of baize. I don't know and offer the suggestion for what it is worth. One author suggests, perhaps more plausibly, that it may be merely a corruption of Bear's Ears.

PUNICA GRANATUM
THE POMEGRANATE

F ALL FRUITS THE POMEGRANATE IS SURELY one of the most romantic. I never know whether I prefer it entire, with its polished leathery rind and oddly flattened sides, or split open, revealing the gleaming pips, each in its watery envelope with the seed visible through the transparency. We can never hope to grow such fully developed fruits in this country, but the tree itself is hardier than usually supposed. It will even flower, producing coral-coloured blossoms among the dark pointed leaves; it will produce miniature fruits in the autumn too, but it is not for the sake of its fruits that I grow it. I grow it for the sake of its leaves and its blossoms; and for the sake, also, of its reddish twigs in spring, and of the young leaves which are as transparent as cornelian against the light before they have properly unfolded. I can think of no other shrub having quite such luminous tips, especially if it is growing above eye-level (as one often sees it on the tops of terrace walls in Italy) so that, looking up as we pass along, we catch it between us and the sun. I give it a warm corner, in the angle formed by a south and east wall; in the winter I heap ashes over its roots, and provide a warm coat in the shape of a

Russian mat tacked across the angle of the two walls. I planted a bush of myrtle beside it, thinking that they went well together both as to appearance and general character, wherein I was indeed right, though it was only some years later that I discovered that some botanists consider the myrtle and the pomegranate to be actually allied. Being no botanist, I had merely remembered the groves of myrtle and pomegranate in which I had slept in Persia.

The pomegranate is a native of Persia and Afghanistan, but has made its way so freely into other countries that it is difficult to say now whether it really grows wild there also or not. Some hold a theory that it has been found in a fossilized state in Pliocene beds in Burgundy, but even without going back to pre-historic times for evidence of its antiquity we can trace a long enough pedigree through history, mythology, literature, and art. It has its name in Sanskrit; it appears in sculpture in Assyria and Egypt; it is mentioned in the Old Testament and the Odyssey. Nausicaa knew it, and her maidens. In Phrygia it shared with the almond the distinction of having enabled the virgin mother of Attis to conceive her mighty son by putting a ripe pomegranate (or almond) into her bosom; in Greece it was held to have sprung from the blood of Dionysos. The Romans got it from Carthage, and called it 'malum punicum' in consequence. The sculptors of the Renaissance, like those of Assyria and Egypt, recognised it as one of the most decorative of fruits – the symbol of poetry and fertility. One really does not know whether to call it romantic or classic: it would provide quite a good starting-point for an argument on those two eternally disputed terms.

VERBASCUM

COTSWOLD VARIETIES

 SUPPOSE EVERY GARDENER IS FAMILIAR
with the Great Mullein (Verbascum thap-
sus), that ubiquitous weed which appears in
likely and unlikely places, sometimes in the
middle of a rich flower-bed, where it will
profit by the good soil to grow three or
four feet in height, sometimes in a starved
dry wall, where it will not attain more than a few inches. It seeds
itself everywhere, and becomes a nuisance and a problem, because
in good conditions it is almost too handsome a weed to root out.
So handsome is it, in fact, with its woolly grey leaves and yellow
spike of bloom, that were it not set down as a weed we should
regard it as a decorative border plant. Besides, considered purely as
a herb, it possesses many varied qualifications. There seems to be
practically no ill which its decoctions will not cure. Mullein tea is
an almost historical remedy for coughs and lung troubles; it is also
reputed to cure such diverse ailments as ringworm, warts,
toothache, headache, earache, and gout. There are also other uses
to which it may be put. It will drive away the evil eye. It will dye
the hair to a rich gold, as Roman women discovered long ago.
Witches made wicks from its leaves for their Sabbaths. Poachers

47

threw its seeds into the water to intoxicate the fish. The poor wore its leaves inside their shoes for warmth. It seems ungrateful to consider so serviceable a plant as a mere weed.

And then again, it goes by so many and such picturesque names in this our country. Some of these names are simply descriptive of the plant and its woolly characteristics: Our Lady's Flannel, or Blanket Herb, or Beggars' Blanket, or Adam's Flannel. There are other names which derive from its practical uses: the Candlewick Plant, or Hag's Taper, with their reference to its utility as tinder when dry. All these considerations ought to add to our tolerance of the Great Mullein when it arises unwanted as a grey and yellow torch in the middle of our carefully planned garden.

Luckily there are some relations of the common mullein which we may legitimately grow as border plants, to be obtained under such names as Verbascum Cotswold Gem or Cotswold Queen. It does not much matter which variety you specify, for they are all equally desirable. They are all dusty, fusty, musty in colouring — queer colours, to which it is impossible to give a definite name: they are neither pink, nor yellow, nor coral, nor apricot, but a cloudy mixture between all those. They look as though a colony of tiny buff butterflies had settled all over them. They are not to be planted in a brilliant garden of orange and scarlet but in some private enclosure where they may associate with other faded colours which will not swear at them or put them to shame. Their flowering season, which is a long one, extends from June into July, therefore they might well be associated with some of the old roses, such as Tuscany or the old Red Damask or the purple Moss.

If only one were as good a gardener in practice as one is in theory, what a garden one would create!

Do not expect your verbascums to do anything much for you during their first year after planting. They will be too busy making roots and leaves to think of throwing up a flower spike, and if they do throw up a flower spike it will be a meagre one, not

worth having, so you had better cut it off and let the plant con-
centrate all its strength for the next season. Be content, for the
first year, with a strong rosette of leaves only, and next year you
can look forward to a group of flowers four feet high. You will
have to stake them, and moreover to stake them early, for they are
very apt to get blown about by any stray wind which may arise.
Four or five sticks and some string will do it, and of course if you
have time to cut off the seeding stalks the more likely you are to
get a second crop. This, I fear, is a counsel of perfection, and I
have very little hope that you will be able to follow my advice.
I proffer it only knowing that it is right, which does not mean that
I follow it myself. There is always so much to be done, that
certain jobs are bound to get neglected. The lupins stand heavy
with seed-pods and so do the delphiniums, but where are the
necessary two, three, four hours to come from? What chance for
the verbascum, who are less showy but more subtle and quite as
deserving?

Dianthus Caesius

THE CHEDDAR PINK

Mid the squander'd colour
　　ilding as I lay
Reading the Odyssey
　　in my rock-garden
I espied the cluster'd
　　tufts of cheddar pinks. . . .

OBERT BRIDGES WAS NOT BEING QUITE accurate in his statements on that occasion, however tenderly he may have expressed his sentiments. His Cheddar Pinks did not grow in a rock-garden at all, but in two long bands down either side of a path at Boar's Hill. At least, that is how I saw them. He may have had them in a rock-garden also, but if so I never saw it. Fortunately for me, the Laureate was not absorbed in the Odyssey that evening, but in an affably hospitable mood was more disposed to exhibit his pinks to an appreciative guest. Dressed in the true Tennysonian tradition in a sort of shepherd's cloak and large black hat, he had already emerged startlingly from among the rhododendrons — or were they laurels? — to open the gate for me on my arrival, and now proposed to extend his courtesy by taking me round his garden. I was charmed, alarmed, and rather overwhelmed. He was so old, so tall, so handsome, so untidy, so noble. And so childishly pleased with his pinks.

They were, indeed, a revelation to me in my ignorance. I had seen them growing wild on the cliffs of the Cheddar Gorge, but had never visualised them massed like this, giving off their scent

so warmly to the summer evening. The Laureate marched in all his stateliness between them, pretending to be less pleased than I could see he was. Every now and then he bent his enormous length to pick some, snapping the stalks very delicately with his sensitive fingers, and having collected a generous bunch he offered it to me, solemnly and even ceremoniously, looking at me very hard meanwhile as though he were sizing me up, which again was an alarming experience. 'They make a pleasant tussie-mussie,' he said as he gave them, and I saw a twinkle in his eye which seemed to indicate that he was testing me on my reception of the unusual word. I was far too much intimidated to suggest that a tussie-mussie really meant a mixed bunch, so I let it go and just said thank you. Looking back, I think he would have liked me better had I bravely corrected him. He would have been amused. One makes these mistakes when one is young and over-anxious to be polite.

Next morning after breakfast he took me into his private room, and read me some passages from a poem he was then writing. He expounded his ideas about its peculiar rhythm in terms so technical as to be completely beyond my comprehension. The poem, when completed, he thought would be called *A* (or possibly *The*) *Testament of Beauty*. Again I was alarmed and overwhelmed. It was altogether too much like meeting the terrifying Tennyson of his old age.

Anyhow, he did introduce me to the virtues of the Cheddar Pink, and I immediately ordered a packet of seed and grew it down my own garden path in the same way, not so much from any desire to imitate the Laureate as from a desire to reproduce that same delicious smell on a warm summer evening. And in doing so I learnt from experience a lesson which the Laureate had omitted to give me. For two summer seasons my Cheddar Pinks were a great success, and I thought they were going on for ever, but, in fact, they had died out. I investigated indignantly and discovered

that our native pink does die out when planted in ordinary garden soil, *i.e.* grown down the edge of an herbaceous border as Dr Bridges was growing it; its only chance of perennial survival is to live in starvation in the crack of a wall, where it may flourish happily year after year. This does not mean that it cannot be grown down the border path also; it means only that you have to renew your supply by fresh seedlings every alternate year – not an excessive trouble to take, when you remember the grey-green clumps which so agreeably throw up the colours of other flowers, and then the pinks themselves while they are blooming and giving off that special, incomparable smell which makes people sniff enquiringly as they wander about your garden.

ROSA MOYESII

HIS IS A CHINESE ROSE, AND LOOKS IT. IF ever a plant reflected all that we had ever felt about the delicacy, lyricism, and design of a Chinese drawing, Rosa Moyesii is that plant. We might well expect to meet her on a Chinese printed paper-lining to a tea-chest of the time of Charles II, when wall-papers first came to England, with a green parrot quite out of all proportions, perching on her slender branches. There would be no need for the artist to stylise her, for Nature has already stylised her enough. Actually, we meet her more often springing out of our English lawns, or overhanging our English streams, yet in whatever corner of our foreign fields, Rosa Moyesii remains for ever China. Yet with that strange adaptability of true genius she never looks out of place. She adapts herself as happily to English brickwork as to the rocks and highlands of Asia.

'Go, lovely rose.' She goes indeed, and quickly. But her beauty is such that she must be grown for the sake of those three weeks in June. During that time her branches will tumble with the large, single, rose-red flower of her being. It is of an indescribable colour. I hold a flower of it here in my hand now, and find myself

defeated in description. It is like the colour I imagine Petra to be,
if one caught it at just the right moment of sunset. It is like some
colours in an especially lovely rug from Isfahan. It is like the dyed
leather sheath of an Arab knife — and this I do know for certain,
for I am matching one against the other, the dagger-sheath against
the flower. It is like all those dusky rose-red things which abide in
the mind as a part of the world of escape and romance.

Then even when the flowers are gone the great graceful branches
are sufficiently lovely in themselves. Consider that within three or
four years a single bush will grow some twelve feet high and will
cover an area six to eight feet wide; long waving wands of leaves
delicately set and of a singularly exquisite pattern, detaching
themselves against the sky or the hedge or the wall, wherever you
happen to have set it. Never make the mistake of trying to train it
tight against a wall: it likes to grow free, and to throw itself
loosely into the fountains of perfect shape it knows so well how
to achieve. Do not, by the way, make the mistake either of indus-
triously cutting off the dead heads, in the hope of inducing a
second flowering. You will not get your second flowering and you
will only deprive yourself of the real second crop which she is
preparing to give you: the crop of long bottle-shaped, scarlet hips
of the autumn. Preserve them at all costs, these sealing-wax fruits
which will hang brighter than the berries of the holly. If you have
a liking for rose-hips, you would be well-advised to mix some
bushes of Highdownensis with your Moyesii, for Highdownensis
(which is in fact a seedling of Moyesii) produces even finer hips —
amongst the finest of any roses in cultivation. And if you are
going in for mixtures, plant Rosa Fargesii too. This is probably
another child of Moyesii, of a lighter and more brilliant shade. I
am never quite sure whether the parent and the child go very well
together, or not. Perhaps not. Perhaps on the whole it would be
better to plant them in separate clumps, with something darkish
to divide them, say rosemary or a couple of Irish yews: the black-

green of the yews would be the ideal background for the precise and delicate luxuriance which the roses will throw up.

Both Fargesii and Highdownensis suggest that Moyesii may produce other children in future. Moyesii has not been for very long in cultivation in European gardens, having been first observed on the Tibetan frontier in 1890, rediscovered in 1903, exhibited in 1908 and put on the market in 1910, so we have as yet had but little time to exploit her possibilities. It seems to be fairly well established that she will not root readily (if at all) from cuttings, so it is evidently on seed that we shall have to depend, and everybody knows how exciting and unexpected seedlings can be. Every amateur among rosegrowers might well make a few experiments.

Even the greatest botanists such as Reginald Farrer derived satisfaction from giving their name to a new plant. It is not given to all of us to find Gentiana Farreri for the first time, but there does seem to be some hope for all of us of raising a new seedling of Rosa Moyesii from our own garden, however humble that garden may be.

ROSA CENTIFOLIA MUSCOSA
THE MOSS ROSE

HERE HAS LATELY BEEN AN ENTHUSIASTIC revival of what we call 'the old roses', to distinguish them from the more fashionable varieties, such as hybrid Teas, hybrid Perpetuals, Polyantha, and Wichuriana. I have no wish to disparage these varieties, which include many very eligible things amongst them, but anyone who falls under the charm of the old roses will seldom find his heart among the newer ones again. This charm may be partly sentimental, and certainly there are several things to be said against the old roses: their flowering time is short; they are untidy growers, difficult to stake or to keep in order; they demand hours of snipping if we are to keep them free from dead and dying heads, as we must do if they are to display their full beauty unmarred by a mass of brown, sodden petals. But in spite of these drawbacks a collection of the old roses gives a great and increasing pleasure. As in one's friends, one learns to overlook their faults and love their virtues.

Having enumerated their faults — or, rather, their disadvantages — what are those virtues? A sentimental association: they recall everything that we have ever read in poetry, or seen in paintings, in connexion with roses. A more personal association, possibly: we may have met them, neglected and ignored in the gardens we knew in childhood. Then, they usually smell better than their modern successors. People complain that the modern rose has lost in smell what it has gained in other ways, and although their accusation is not always justified there is still a good deal of truth in it. No such charge can be brought against the Musk, the Cabbage, the Damask, of the Moss. They load the air with the true rose scent.

The Musk may excel the Moss in this respect, but since the Moss is only a form of the Cabbage it shares the deep, velvety scent of its relation, with the added attraction of its own furry calices and shoots. Nobody knows when first a Cabbage rose turned itself into a Moss, but the first gardener to observe the freak must certainly have thought with alarm that his bushes were affected by some unknown disease. And so, in a sense, they were. Mr E. Bunyard who has done so much to restore the old roses to current favour, puts it neatly in his book, *Old Garden Roses*, 'The moss is a proliferation of the glands which are always present in the Cabbage roses.' Proliferation was an unfamiliar word to me, although the context showed me what Mr Bunyard meant, but on looking it up in the dictionary, I arrived at the more precise meaning: Proliferate: reproduce itself, grow by multiplication of elementary parts; so, proliferation. Well, the Moss rose as we know it has proliferated itself from the Cabbage by a multiplication of the elementary parts or glands. It seems a dry and rather medical way of putting it, but how lucky for us that the freak became fixed into a permanent and enchanting form.

Some rosarians cling firmly to the maxim that the rose which fades from red to lilac is a bad rose, an undesirable rose, a rose instantly to be abolished from our gardens; but others, less conventionally-minded, hold that the bishop's-purple of its dying hours invests it with a second beauty. In the case of the Moss, we

must agree. I have in my garden two bushes of the Moss, William Lobb (incidentally they have attained a height of twelve feet), and as they reach the stage where some of the flowers are passing while others are still coming out, they look as though some rich ecclesiastical vestment had been flung over them. The dull carnation of the fresh flowers accords so perfectly with the slaty lilac of the old, and the bunches cluster in such profusion, that the whole bush becomes a cloth of colour, sumptuous, as though stained with blood and wine. If they are to be grown in a border, I think they should be given some grey-leaved plant in front of them, such as Stachys lanata (more familiarly, Rabbits' Ears), for the soft grey accentuates their own musty hues, but ideally speaking, I should like to see a small paved garden with grey stone walls given up to them entirely, with perhaps a dash of the old rose called Veilchenblau climbing the walls and a few clumps of the crimson clove carnation at their feet.

ROSA MUNDI

HE WARS OF THE ROSES BEING FORTUNATELY over, making one war the less for us to reckon with, we are left to the simple enjoyment of the flower which traditionally symbolises that historic contest. The only question is, which rose are we really to regard as the true York-and-Lancaster? For the one which most people hail cheerfully by that name in gardens very often turns out to be not York-and-Lancaster at all, but Rosa Mundi.

There is no adequate reason why this confusion should have arisen, for apart from the fact that they both have variegated petals, the two roses are not really very much alike. The Rose of the World (Rosa Mundi) is a Gallica, the Rose of the Wars (York-and-Lancaster) a Damask, but in case that classification is not of much practical use to you, here are two other ways by which you may tell them. York-and-Lancaster is a very pale pink, almost white; a few petals are variegated, but not all; a washy thing, not worth having. Rosa Mundi is far more striking. She is of a deeper pink, and *all* the petals are stained with a true carmine. She is also far more free-flowering. It does not very much matter if people, wrongly, like to go on calling her York-and-Lancaster, as they always do and no doubt always will. What matters is that we can now buy a rose which is variously called Rosa Mundi or York-and-Lancaster by the ignorant, and so long as we are quite sure in our mind that it is Rosa Mundi we have chosen, can depend upon getting something which will increase in luxuriance from year to year. Striped and splotched and blotted, this fine old rose explodes into florescence in June, giving endless variations of her markings. You never know what form these markings are going to take. Sometimes they come in red orderly stripes, some-times in splashes, sometimes in mere stains and splotches, but always various, decorative, and interesting. They remind one rather of red cherry juice generously stirred into a bowl of cream. A bush of Rosa Mundi in full flowering is worth looking at. It is not worth cutting for the house, unless you have the leisure to renew your flower-vases every day, for in water it will not last. Even out of doors, blooming on its own bush, it does not last for very long. It is a short-lived delight, but during the short period of its blooming it makes up in quantity what it lacks in durability. It gives the best of itself for about a fortnight, and then it seems to have expended its total effort for the whole year.

Perhaps all the foregoing makes it sound rather unsatisfactory and not worth while. On the contrary, it is very much worth while indeed. For one thing, you can stick it in any odd corner, and indeed you will be wise to do so, unless you have a huge garden where you can afford blank gaps during a large part of the year. You can also grow it as a hedge, down any path which you habitually use in your garden, and let it ramp away. Mix some moss roses with it, and you will soon have a rose-hedge so thick and romantic that all the nightingales of the neighbouring woods will come to press their breasts in song against the thorns. But the companion which really suits it best is Tuscany, who gets a section to herself in this book.

A word as to pruning. The true York-and-Lancaster scarcely needs any pruning at all, except at the interval of a few years, when the bush threatens to become straggly. Rosa Mundi, on the other hand, needs all weak shoots to be cut out after the flowering time is over, and in the spring the remaining shoots should be shortened to within half a dozen buds.

A further word as to suckers, those long, strong, thorny growths which most healthy roses throw up from the base of the bush, and which must be cut away unless the bush is to revert entirely to the original briar (or wild rose) stock on which it has been budded. It is sometimes difficult to decide whether the new shoot is a sucker or a valuable fresh addition supplied by the rose itself. Roughly speaking, a sucker springs from below ground-level (*i.e.* it springs from the *root* of the rose), and this, although not conclusive, is always an indication that the shoot should be regarded with suspicion. The sucker will usually be found to carry larger and more vicious thorns than the rose proper, and the leaves, if closely examined, will be found to differ. The most useful hint of all was given to me verbally by Mr Bunyard — one of those simple rules which for some reason are never to be found in books, 'Remember,' he said, 'that a sucker can never have more than seven leaves on a single stalk, and that therefore any shoot bearing more than seven leaves cannot possibly be a sucker.'

ROSA GALLICA
TUSCANY

I FEAR THAT MY CHOICE AMONG THE OLD roses may be regarded as somewhat arbitrary and limited. Limited it admittedly is, and I regret it. There is scarcely a variety I should not have liked to discuss, from the tight and tiny De Meaux to the lyrically named Cuisse de Nymphe Émue, but a sense of apportionment forbade it. I could not put in too many roses to the exclusion of other flowers, and this is why I have restricted myself to Rosa Mundi, the Moss Rose, and the Gallica Rose called Tuscany.

There seems to have existed once a rose known as the Velvet Rose. Nobody knows with any certainty what particular rose was meant by this name, but it is supposed that it must have been a Gallica. Nobody knows the place of its origin: was it truly a wilding in Europe, or had it been imported into cultivation from the East? These are mysteries which have not as yet been resolved. All that we can say is that the name is very descriptive of its supposed descendants, amongst which we must include my favourite Tuscany.

The Velvet Rose. What a combination of words! One almost

suffocates in their soft depths, as though one sank into a bed of rose-petals, all thorns ideally stripped away. We cannot actually lie on a bed of roses, unless we are very decadent and also very rich, but metaphorically we can imagine ourselves doing so when we hold a single rose close to our eyes and absorb it in an intimate way into our private heart. This sounds a fanciful way of writing, the sort of way which makes me shut up most gardening books with a bang, but in this case I am trying to get as close to my true meaning as possible. It really does teach one something, to look long and closely into a rose, especially such a rose as Tuscany, which opens flat (being only semi-double) thus revealing the quivering and dusty gold of its central perfection.

Tuscany is more like the heraldic Tudor rose than any other. The petals, of the darkest crimson, curl slightly inwards and the anthers, which are of a rich yellow, shiver and jingle loosely together if one shakes the flower.

As, like Rose Mundi, Tuscany is a Gallica, it needs the same kind of pruning; it will never make a very tall bush, and your effort should be to keep it shapely — not a very easy task, for it tends to grow spindly shoots, which must be rigorously cut out. Humus and potash benefit the flowers and the leaves respectively.

ABUTILON
MEGAPOTAMICUM
OR
VEXILLARIUM

 HIS CURIOUS BRAZILIAN CLIMBER WITH the formidable name is usually offered as a half-hardy or greenhouse plant, but experience shows that it will withstand as many degrees of frost as it is likely to meet within the southern counties. It is well worth trying against a south wall, for apart from the unusual character of its flowers it has several points to recommend it. For one thing it occupies but little space, seldom growing more than four feet high, so that even if you should happen to lose it you will not be left with a big blank gap. For another, it has the convenient habit of layering itself of its own accord, so that by merely separating the rooted layers and putting them into the safety of a cold frame, you need never be without a supply of substitutes. For another, it is apt to flower at times when you least expect it which always provides an amusing surprise.

You should thus grow it somewhere you are constantly likely to pass and can glance at it daily to see what it is doing without having to go out of your way. Another reason for doing this is that it is not one of those showy climbers which you can see from

the other side of the garden, but requires to be looked at as closely as though you were short-sighted. And you can only do so in the open, for if you cut it to bring into the house it will be dead within the hour, which is unsatisfactory both for it and for you. But sitting on the grass at the foot of the wall where it grows, you can stare up into the queer hanging bells and forget what the people round you are saying. It is not an easy flower to describe – no flower is, but the Abutilon is particularly difficult. In despair I turned up its botanically official description: 'Ls. lanc., 3, toothed. Fls. $1^1/_2$, sepals red, petals yellow, stamens long and drooping (like a fuchsia)'.

Now in the whole of that laconic though comprehensive description there were only three words which could help me at all: like a fuchsia. And of course I had thought of them already. The flower of the Abutilon *is* like a fuchsia, both in size and in shape, though not in colour. I know that it is no use ever hoping that anybody else will see precisely the same comparisons as one does oneself, unless they are very obvious, but both the fuchsia and the Abutilon always remind me of the Russian ballet. 'Sepals red, petals yellow' is translated for me into a tight-fitting red bodice with a yellow petticoat springing out below it in flares, a coloured and neat little figure, which could twirl on the point of the stamens as on the point of the toes. One can, in fact, almost spin it like a top.

Abutilon megapotamicum has a companion, Abutilon vitifolium, which is more frequently grown, but which is less interesting – at least, according to my taste – with its pale mauve flowers or their white variety.

PRIMULA PULVERULENTA
THE BARTLEY STRAIN

HE EARLY YEARS OF THIS CENTURY, WHICH introduced such an amazing crop of new treasures to English gardens, produced amongst other discoveries from Western China the Primula known as pulverulenta — the powdered or mealy primula. It rapidly and rightly became a favourite, but to my mind at least its crimson head is a crude thing compared with the delicate refinement of the Bartley strain which is its child. Mr G. H. Dalrymple, who bred the Bartley strain, has been kind enough to furnish me with an account of how it came into being:

'Among the first plants of P. pulverulenta raised in this country there appeared a pale pink sport . . . I was so great-ly taken with this plant and was so anxious to own it that I tried hard to get seed as plants were then (1912) very expen-sive . . . I had to use the pollen of the type plant on the pink sport to get seed, and the resulting seedlings gave me ninety-nine per cent type colour and one plant that flow-ered pink. After some years of work on it I had increased the percentage of pink flowers appearing in each generation

until 1921 when the drought killed off every plant except one which produced a few seeds. From these I had about one hundred seedlings to plant out . . . and the following spring I had about fifty per cent pink. Further selecting, and the next generation gave me a better percentage and from these I selected the best and started another generation which gave me I might say ninety-nine per cent pink shades. Another selection, and the type plant completely disappeared and has never appeared since.'

The uninitiated may be surprised at the years of patience required before any new flower is triumphantly put upon the market, but Mr Dalrymple's primula is so lovely, as to reward him now for any trouble he took to secure it. In its habit of growth, P. pulverulenta resembles P. japonica, rising in a straight stem from amongst a cluster of leaves, and then displaying itself in ring upon ring of flowers. Against the white floury stem as soft to the look as fur is to the touch, you must imagine the rings of pink, in perfectly toned association. It is difficult to give any exact idea of the colour in words; to compare it with the pink of peach-blossom would be to suggest something far too crude, with the pink of apple-blossom something far too washy, with the pink of a sunset-cloud something far too pink; nor is there any rose which will give me the precise shade I want. It really suggests a far deeper pink which has been dusted over with chalk, so that the original colour shows through, behind the slight veil which has been powdered over it by a puff or a breath of wind.

There is a way of growing this primula which will greatly enhance the beautiful straightness of the stems. You should set it on a steep low bank, so that it appears to rise in tiers of increasing heights. Thus, the plants towards the top will tower two to three feet above the ones at the bottom, creating a sheet of chalky pink, sloping down and far more effective than an equal mass of

uniform height. At the top of the bank I suggest azaleas of suitable colour; and there are many.

Only one difficulty presents itself against this plan. It is the simple difficulty that steep banks usually mean natural drainage, and that these primulas prefer to grow in places which retain coolness and moisture throughout the summer. Therefore you must be quite sure that your steep bank is as cool and damp at the top as at the bottom, otherwise they will thrive in the lower reaches and die parched at the top. This sounds an impossibly ideal condition to impose, but you can fulfil it if your garden offers a bank facing north, well-shaded by trees which protect from the blistering sun. Then both your azaleas and primulas can hide themselves from the mid-day glare; can flower happily, unparched, unscorched; and can ripen and develop towards another year.

A warning: should you wish to save the seed off your own plants, be careful that the mice do not take it before you do. Pulverulenta is the only primula which a mouse will attack in this way.

PRIMULA LITTONIANA

HE AMATEUR GARDENER DOES NOT AS A rule trouble his head very much with botanical groupings. Such names as 'scrophulariceæ' and 'crassulaceæ' merely inspire him with boredom and distaste. Yet I suppose that a few of the natural orders are instantly recognisable, and that to the roses and lilies we may safely add the great family of the primulaceæ. Lacking it, we should be without the primrose, the cowslip, the auricula, the polyanthus, and the innumerable varieties of primula.

The absence of the primrose and the polyanthus alone, with their range of colours, would impoverish the spring garden perhaps more than we realise. Consider that we can now grow them in blue, mauve, magenta, yellow, white, ruby, bronze, orange; consider also that they spread their flowering over nearly two months in April and May; that even in autumn and throughout a mild winter you are liable to find a few stray blooms; that they may be increased indefinitely, either by self-sown seedlings or by pulling big clumps to pieces. There are few plants more obliging. The smallest rooted bit will grow, and it is even possible to transplant them while in full flower: they scarcely seem to notice the

move. A cool soil and the same amount of shade as pleases our native primrose are all they ask.

Their grander relations, the tall primulas, vary of course in amiability. They are the aristocrats of the group and as such are entitled to their fancies. Some of them, indeed, appear to be so democratically-minded as to accommodate themselves to our wishes as readily as the primrose and the polyanthus; thus, although P. Japonica and the yellow P. Sikkimensis have travelled across half the world before reaching England, they give themselves no airs on arrival but adapt themselves happily to the banks of our woodland streams, set a lavish store of seed for our use, and quickly grow themselves into dividable clumps as big as cabbages. With these, however, I am not for the moment concerned. I am concerned with the more unusual Primula Littoniana, a native of Yunnan, which many people admire when they see it at flower-shows but seldom grow in their own gardens. It seems to be one of those plants which get so far as the compliment of an X pencilled against it in the nurseryman's leaflet, and stop at that. I do not quite know why. It is a very shapely thing, not difficult to grow with success. The conditions under which this primula likes to be grown are cool, shady, rather moist, with plenty of leaf-mould for its rather shallow root-run, and protection from a burning sun. Given these, a colony should flourish, but do not expect to be able to increase it by seed for it is not at all obliging in that respect. Your only hope is to increase by division of a sturdy plant.

Mutisia Retusa

UTISIA RETUSA DOES NOT SEEM TO HAVE advanced very far in popularity since its recent arrival from Chile, but I think that must be because few amateur gardeners know of it as yet. It takes several years to become properly established, so that comparatively few people have plants old enough to display its mature beauty, otherwise it would surely have leapt into every garden, for such a plant, once seen, is enough to stir envy and consequent emulation.

It is a climber, with starry pink flowers rather like the flowers of a clematis, neither garish, nor startling, but borne in great profusion. For the first two or three years after planting, it will produce scarcely and flowers at all, and those that it does produce will be meagre, disappointing, and rather spiky compared with the fuller and more rounded petals that will follow with increasing age. Like wine, the Mutisia improves as it grows older. It needs time to mellow. Do not root it out in disappointment while it is still young. Rather, forget about it until one day in some July it surprises you by a cloud of pink thrown wildly over the tree at whose foot you have planted it.

For you must plant it at the foot of some tree you are prepared to sacrifice. Mutisia retusa does not like being trained tidily against a wall; it likes to wreathe its way upwards through branches and to lace itself in and out until it reaches the sunlight and can crawl over every twig of its host with its remarkably prehensile tendrils. Obviously, this is not good for the host although it may be ideal for the guest, and therefore you must choose a tree whose loss you will not regret. An old apple or pear will serve the purpose well; or, better still, an unesteemed Irish yew of the size and shape seen in country churchyards. If you have one of these growing in some stray corner of the garden, and think it too dismal (as some people do, though I cannot agree) then plant Mutisia retusa beside it and turn its dark-green gloom into a wreathing, strangling mass of starred pink petals. The dark green of the yew, almost black, shows up the virginal pink of the climber; they look like a living parable of age and youth.

That great gardener, William Robinson, generously understood the secret of growing one plant into another. It was as though he adapted the system of the tropical forests he had never seen, to the possibilities of an English garden. He could not fling orchids towards the sun on the tops of high trees, but he could and did fling festoons of roses and clematis right up into his English trees, so that they hung in surprising places, high up, where the conventional grower never thought to look for them. I wonder what he would have made of Mutisia retusa? He would undoubtedly have thrown it up into the air somewhere, to return towards earth in a blanket of pink over precisely the dark back-cloth it demanded.

Lilium Regale

HE DEBT THAT WE STAY-AT-HOME GARDENERS in comfortable England owe to brave botanists who risk their lives in dangerous territories can scarcely be over-estimated. It is all very well for us private gardeners to wait, safely and snugly, for the seeds or bulbs of hitherto unknown plants to take their place in the catalogues of nurserymen; we are apt to forget, or to overlook, the efforts which have made such purchases possible. We forget the adventures, the dangers, the hardships, which men have willingly experienced in order to enrich us casual purchasers of their spoils. We forget the preparations for expeditions, the struggle to engage native porters, mules, packs, and what not, the long trek over difficult tracks, the alarming nights and days, the frequent poises between life and death, the unique and thrilling moment when after all this cost of courage and endurance, the reward is suddenly found in a flower hitherto unknown to European eyes. What a moment for the collector, when after all his pains and expense and trouble he stumbles almost by chance on some unlooked for prize – a moment comparable almost to a mathematical discovery or to writing a

line of great poetry, for when he works on this high plane of adventure the seeker of new flowers begins to take rank with the creative artist.

We now, in 1937, accept Lilium regale, the regal lily, as a commonplace of our English gardens, forgetting that only so recently as 1905 was she discovered in Western China by Dr Ernest Wilson. The bulbs were scarce and remained expensive for several years, but owing to the ease with which the regal lily may be grown from seed, only two or three years being needed to produce a flowering bulb, the nurserymen's prices rapidly came down and the bulbs may now be obtained for a few pence. Many amateurs sow their own seed, which will germinate as freely as mustard and cress. Nature is the neatest of packers, and each seed-pod is arranged with thousands of tiny wafers, laid one above the other with exquisite precision, so that if you are prepared to go to the trouble of sowing and pricking out you can grow acres of regale with no expense at all.

Once arrived at maturity regale must be admitted as one of the most satisfactory of all lilies. Three feet is a good height for her to attain, and she will carry as many as thirteen or fourteen of the white trumpets (though the more normal number is five or six) whose exterior is flushed with wine-pink and whose interior is stained with a buttercup yellow. Three feet may easily be exceeded, and amateurs will tell you proudly of two dozen trumpets on a single stem. The scent is as strong as that of Lilium auratum – so strong, that one or two in a room is enough for most people. She is not particular as to aspect, for although she is commonly supposed to prefer full sun, and although in her native home of the Min Valley she 'luxuriates in rocky crevices, sun-baked throughout the greater part of the year', I have also seen her growing happily on the north side of a high wall. The only danger which seems to threaten her is that of late frosts, and in a disastrous frost we experienced a few years ago in May the young stems

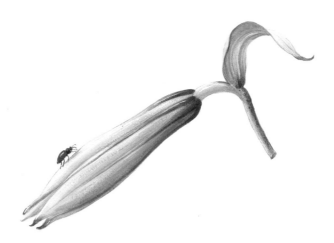

were curled limply over and blackened in the night. The bulbs were uninjured, but there were no flowers that year. The moral is, throw down some bracken if hard weather seems likely: or, as an alternative, grow your lilies where they will have the protection of some low shrubby plant such as a dwarf lavender.

Lilium Giganteum

T IS A CONTRAST TO TURN FROM THE SMALL delicacies of my painters' flowers and from the embroidery of the old roses, to the towering heroism of the Himalayan lily. Too splendid to be called vulgar, she is still very decidedly over life-size. Unconsciously, one sets oneself some kind of limit as to what size a flower ought to be, and here is one which exceeds them all. It looks almost as though she had adapted herself to the proportions of her tremendous home. For I suppose that there is no scenery in the world so appallingly majestic as that of the great mountains of Central Asia. Farrer found her in Tibet, and any reader of his books will have formed some distant idea of that remote and lonely region, scarcely travelled and practically unmapped, where men are few, but flowers are many, a ravishing population put there as it were to compensate for the rudeness of life, the violence of the climate, and the desolation of the ranges.

So the Giant Lily, not to be outdone, has matched her stature against the great fissures and precipices and nameless peaks. In an English garden she looks startling indeed, but out there a peculiar fitness must attend her, making of her the worthy and

proportionate ornament, sculptural as she is with her long, quiet
trumpets and dark, quiet leaves. I do not know to what height
she will grow in her native home, but in England she will reach
twelve feet without much trouble, and I have heard it said that in
Scotland she will reach eighteen.

A group of these lilies, seen by twilight or moonlight gleaming
under the shadow of a thin wood, is a truly imposing sight. The
scent is overpowering, and seems to be the only expression of life
vouchsafed by these sentinels which have so strange a quality of
stillness. I should like to see them growing among silver birches,
whose pale trunks would accord with the curious greenish-white
trumpets of the flower-spike. Unluckily, we have not all got a
birch-wood exactly where we want it; and even though we were
willing to make a plantation, the stem of the young birch lacks the
quality of the old. Alders would do well; they have the requisite
pallor and ghostliness.

But failing either of these, any coppice say of hazel or chestnut
will serve the purpose, which is to provide shade and coolness, for
the Giant Lily will stand a good deal of both. Then you must
dig out a hole two to three feet deep, and fill it with the richest
material you can provide in the form of leaf-mould, peat, and
rotted manure. This simple recommendation reminds me of the
exclamation of a friend: 'It seems to me,' she said, 'that this lily of
yours has all the virtues and only four disadvantages: it is very
expensive to buy; the bulk takes three years before it flowers; after
flowering once it dies; and you have to bury a dead horse at the
bottom of a pit before it will flower at all.'

Up to a point, these remarks are true. A bulb of flowering size
does cost five shillings, it does then die, and it does demand a lot
of feeding. On the other hand it will produce a number of
bulblets which you can grow on for yourself, thus arranging for an
inexhaustible stock. The best plan is to buy as many three-year old
bulbs as you can afford, and also some second year bulbs which

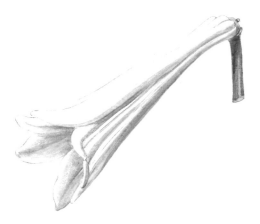

are cheaper. By the time your second year bulbs have flowered and died, you will have some third year bulbs ready for your own raising, and then you are safe indefinitely.

Having then dug your hole in October and filled it up again, you plant the bulbs so shallowly that the tip, or nose, just shows above the surface of the ground. It is wise to throw down some covering of leaves or bracken as a protection against late frosts. It is wise also to put in some tall stakes at the same time as you do the planting, for stakes will be needed, and by ramming them in later on you run the risk of damaging roots or even the bulb itself. When the leaves begin to appear in spring, put down slug-bait for the slugs attack with vigour, and the glossy perfection of the huge leaves is a thing to be jealously guarded. You then wait for June, when you may expect your reward.

In the following October, of course, you dig up the old bulbs and throw them away, having first carefully saved the bulblets which you will find clustering round it like chicks round a hen.

ZINNIAS

 NTHOLOGISTS SOMETIMES TAKE ESPECIAL
delight in quoting the botanical howlers
made by reputable authors, but (unless I
have overlooked it, which is quite likely), no
anthologist has yet put his finger on Walter
Pater's howler when in *Marius the Epicurean* he
makes his Romans go in search of zinnias
wherewith to deck themselves. 'They visited the flower-market,
lingering where the *coronarii* pressed on them the newest species,
and purchased zinias (sic) now in blossom (like painted flowers,
thought Marius), to decorate the folds of their togas.' Now either
Pater had some botanical information drawn from Roman histori-
ans and subsequently mislaid by us, or else he was merely drawing
on his imagination to find a flower which he thought suitable to
decorate a toga. If he was just drawing on his imagination, he
went absurdly wrong. For as the zinnia is a native of America and
Mexico, and as Marius lived in Rome in the 2nd century A.D.
Pater is out by about twelve centuries: he was, in fact, enriching
Rome by a flower from a continent not due for discovering until
some twelve hundred years later. I suppose this must be granted
under the heading poetic licence.

In actual fact, the original zinnia, or Zinnia elegans, was intro-
duced into European countries in 1796, and since then has been
'improved' into the garden varieties we now know and grow. Many
flowers lose by this so-called improvement; the zinnia has gained.
Some people call it artificial-looking, and so in a way it is. It
looks as though it had been cut out of bits of cardboard inge-
niously glued together into the semblance of a flower. It is prim
and stiff and arranged and precise, almost geometrically precise,
so that many people who prefer the more romantic, lavish flowers
reject it just on account of its stiffness and regularity. 'Besides,'
they say, and rightly, 'it gives us a lot of trouble to grow. It is only
half-hardy in this country, and thus has to be sown in a seed-box
under glass in February or March; pricked out; and then planted
out in May where we want it to flower. We have to be very careful
not to water the seedlings too much, or they will damp off and
die. Then, when we have planted it out, we have to be on the
look-out for slugs which have for zinnias an affection greatly
exceeding our own. Why should we take all this trouble about
growing a flower which we know is going to be cut down by the
first autumn frost?'

Such arguments crash like truncheons, and it takes an effort to renew our determination by recalling the vivid bed which gave us weeks of pleasure last year. For there are few flowers more brilliant without being crude, and since they are sun-lovers the hot dry spot where we plant them will shower the maximum of light on the formal heads and array of colours. Whether we grow them in a mixture (sold, I regret to say, under the description 'art shades') or separate the pink from the orange, the red from the magenta, is a matter of taste. Personally I like them higgledy-piggledy, when they look like those pats of paint squeezed out upon the palette, and I like them all by themselves, not associated with anything else.

As cut flowers they are invaluable: they never flop, and they last I was going to say for weeks.

TIGRIDIAS
THE TIGER-FLOWER

'May be grown with success on a hot, dry border.'

HIS IS TYPICAL OF THE INSTRUCTIONS GIVEN in gardening books and nurserymen's catalogues, which make the Englishman ask himself where he is going to find a hot dry border in this country. Borders, as he well knows, are more apt to be chilly owing to the deficiency of sun, and wet owing to the excess of rain. He thinks with envy of those strips of soil at the foot of Provençal terraces, which might well be described as hot and dry, and, as such, fit homes for such sun-lovers as the Mexican Tiger-Flower. He thinks of that succession of blazing days, interrupted only by an occasional thunderstorm. (Thus do we idealise climates other than our own, and forget the disadvantages against which we do not have to contend.)

He may, however, take heart, for there are several ways in which he may improvise or at any rate substitute conditions such as those recommended. It is true that he cannot provide sunshine when the sun refuses to shine, but he can at least choose his border where any available sunshine will strike it, facing either south or east; and he can do a great deal towards the desirable dryness. He can arrange for dryness, *i.e.* good drainage, either by making his border on the sharp slope of a hill, or by raising it several inches above the natural level of flat ground on a bed banked up by a stone (or brick) surround, with a foundation of broken rubble or ashes under the soil. Both these systems entail trouble and labour. Far more simply, he can walk round his house and find a narrow strip of border facing south or east, which is almost entirely protected from rain by the over-hanging eaves of the house. In such a position, only such summer rain as is driven in by an accompanying wind ever reaches the six or eight inches at the foot of the house-wall; and this, provided the soil is sufficiently light and crumbly, is an ideal position in which to grow tigridias.

I imagine, therefore, a long narrow bed under the shelter of the eaves, entirely given up to this brilliant and ephemeral flower. Let me explain these two adjectives. Brilliant is frequently used of flowers too rashly and too unadvisedly, but of the tigridia with deserved justice, for a border of these Mexicans really resembles a colony of bright and enormous insects, settled upon green leaves but ready at any moment to be off. They look like gigantic butterflies, flat, open, wing-spread; white, yellow, orange, carmine, spotted, speckled, beautifully shaped. But ephemeral, short-lived. One would expect no less of such a butterfly flower. Within a few hours of opening, the individual flower has closed its petals in a saddened droop. Watching them, it seems tragic that so exquisite a form of creation should also be so wasteful, that the surprising bloom which one has discovered in the morning should be gone by the afternoon; but in splendid compensation another crop of poised insects is there next morning, like a renewal of reward after brief discouragement.

The moral of all this is that the tiger-iris (for tigridias belong to the iris family) should be planted in dozens or in hundreds. Only by planting a quantity can you ensure a real display. Each plant will give generously, but it takes a quantity to keep up the daily, hourly supply. Like dahlias or gladioli, they had better be

TIGRIDIAS

taken up for the winter and kept in a shed where the frost will not injure them; but unlike dahlias or gladioli, they give no trouble as to staking, for they grow low to the ground, a great advantage over those more usual and obvious flowers, which are to be found in every garden, where tigridias are not.

GERBERA JAMESONII
THE TRANSVAAL DAISY

HERE ARE SOME FLOWERS ABOUT WHICH there is nothing interesting to say, except that they happen to have caught one's fancy. Such a flower, so far as I am concerned, is Gerbera Jamesonii. It has no historical interest that I know of; no long record of danger and difficulty attending its discovery; no background of savage mountains and Asiatic climates. It carries, in fact, no romantic appeal at all. It has taken no man's life. It has to stand or fall on its own merits.

I first observed it in the window of a florist's shop, neatly rising out of a gilt basket tied with pink ribbons. No more repellant presentation could be imagined, or anything more likely to put one against the flower for ever, yet somehow this poor ill-treated flower struck me instantly as a lovely thing, so lovely that I suffered on its behalf to see it so misunderstood. I went in to enquire its name, but the young lady assistant merely gaped at me, as they nearly always do if one makes any enquiry about their wares unconnected with their price. It was only later, at a flower-show, that I discovered it to be Gerbera Jamesonii, also called the Transvaal daisy. Neither name pleased me very much, but the

flower itself pleased me very much indeed. It seemed to include every colour one could most desire, especially a coral pink and a rich yellow, and every petal as shiny and polished as a buttercup. Long, slender stalks and a clean erect habit. It was altogether a very clean looking flower; in fact it might have been freshly varnished.

The exhibitor was better informed than the florist's young lady. It was only hardy in this country, he said, if it could be grown in very dry conditions at the foot of a warm wall, in which case it might be regarded as a reasonably hardy perennial. I know however that nurserymen are frequently more optimistic in their recommendations than they should be, so privately resolved to grow it in an unheated greenhouse. This house is really a long lean-to, sloped against the brick wall of an old stable, and all along the foot of the wall runs a bed about six feet wide, which is an ideal place for growing things such as the Gerbera which cannot without a certain anxiety be left out-of-doors. I wonder indeed why those who are fortunate enough to possess such a lean-to do not more frequently put it to this use. It is true that it entails sacrificing all the staging down one side of the house, but the gain is great. Staging means pots, and pots mean watering, and 'potting on' if you are to avoid root starvation, whereas plants set straight into the ground can root down to Australia if they like. You can moreover make up the soil to suit every separate kind; you can work under cover in bad weather; you can snap your fingers at hailstorms, late frosts, young rabbits, and even, to a certain extent, slugs. There is certainly a great deal to be said for this method of gardening.

I once saw a lean-to house which had been adapted in this way, with a special view to growing lilies. The wall had been distempered a light blue, of that peculiar shade produced by spraying vines with copper sulphate against the walls of farm-houses in Italy: in the centre was a sunk rectangular pool, with

blue nympheæ growing in it and clumps of agapanthus at each of the four corners. The tall lilies rose straight and pure and pale against the curious blue of the wall. I liked best going into this house after dark, when the single electric reflector in the roof cast down a flood-lighting effect more unreal and unearthly than anything I had ever seen.

At least, let me be strictly truthful, I never really saw this lean-to house at all. I only heard it discussed, before it had materialised. And then it grew in my mind, turning into the thing I wanted it to be. In my mind, I added the pool, and the spraying with copper sulphate, and the flood-lighting, and the pale lilies. It was ideally lovely, as I imagined it. Perhaps it has materialised since then, perhaps it has not. I almost hope it has not.

SALPIGLOSSIS

OONER OR LATER ONE HAS TO MAKE UP ONE'S mind as to whether half-hardy annuals are worth growing or not. They certainly take up a lot of time, and once the frost has cut them down they are gone for ever, and all our labour with them, for, unlike the hardy annual, they will not renew themselves in their self-sown children the following year. It is of course possible to diminish the labour, by sowing the seeds in the open garden at the end of April or beginning of May, instead of following the orthodox method of sowing in boxes under glass in the autumn or very early spring, but then one has to take the risk of a late frost which may blacken an entire bed of young plants in one night. On the whole it is better to stick to the safe and orthodox way, with all its attendant pricking off and planting out. Every autumn I solemnly resolve that this shall really be the last time I treat myself to such luxuries, and every summer when I see the results of my trouble I revoke my resolution. I have, however, reached the stage of limiting my choice to the very few half hardies which I cannot be without. Among these, the zinnia and the salpiglossis hold a high place.

The salpiglossis arrived in this country from Chile as long ago
as 1820 and is one of those flowers which has benefited incredibly
from the attentions of horticulturists to the original form. There
is now nothing which is not entirely lovely about it except its name.
I wish it could acquire a decent English name, instead of this
corrupt Greek (from *salpigx*, trumpet, and *glossa*, tongue), but if it
possesses an English name I never heard it. Perhaps when it has
been with us for another century the constant mis-pronunciations
to which it is subjected will produce an unrecognisable variant, for
there are few botanical names which give greater trouble in the
arrangement of their vowels and consonants. It seems necessary
for the English tongue to put in an additional p or s somewhere.
I have never heard it called 'salpiglopsis' and 'salsipiglossis' alter-
nately, both, unfortunately, even more hideous than their original.
I wonder what it is called in Chile?

Its name apart, it is, as I said, entirely lovely. To my mind it far
exceeds its relation the petunia in every way. The range and
richness of its colour is amazing. You can grow it in purple and
gold, or in ruby and gold, or in white and gold, when it has the
milky purity, gold-embroidered, which one traditionally associates
with the robes of saints and angels. Then you can also grow it in

brown and gold, a very rare colour in flowers, for it is a true brown – the brown of corduroy, with all the depth of the velvet pile. The illustration clearly shows the veining drawn as though by the stroke of a fine brush; and moreover suggests what is actually the truth; that the salpiglossis shows to great advantage as a cut flower. Out in the garden it is apt to look bedraggled rather too easily, for unless it has been carefully staked its brittle stems suffer badly from wind or heavy rain, but in a vase its intense livery glows unsullied. Place it for choice in a window or on a table where the sun will strike it, and then ask yourself whether it has not proved itself worthy of all the care it entailed.

For the same reason, try growing it as pot-plant for the winter months. It adapts itself very graciously to this treatment. Of course you must keep it warm: forty to fifty degrees should be a safe temperature. In fact, you might try rescuing half a dozen plants from the garden in the autumn before the frosts come, potting them, and seeing whether they would not carry on, getting even sturdier as they grew older. I have never tried this scheme myself, but I see no reason why it should not meet with success. I have done it with other things, so why not with the salpiglossis? Experiments are always interesting, but if you prefer the safer course sow a few seeds in pots in September and grow them on in what gardeners descriptively call a gentle heat.

LILIUM AURATUM

 HE VARIOUS LILIES PRESENT A PROBLEM TO the amateur gardener. The advice offered to him by gardening books, nurserymen, and personal friends alternates between divergence and unanimity of opinion, both of which his own experience will prove to be wrong. He is told to plant shallow, and to plant deep; to supply manure and to avoid manure at all costs; to provide shade, and to choose the sunniest site possible. The Madonna lily (Lilium candidum) perhaps gives rise to the oddest combination of contradictions between divergence and unanimity. On the divergent side we are told (a) that the Madonna lily revels in a heavy mulch of manure, and (b) that manure is the one thing she cannot abide. We are told (a) to plant her among other growing things, that her roots may be shaded; (b) to plant her where the hot sun will ripen her bulbs. We are told (c) to lift the bulbs every two or three years; (d) never, at our peril, to move the bulbs at all. On the unanimous side we are told that the Madonna lily is the easiest of all lilies to grow with complete success, and that, as every gardener who has not the luck to be a cottager knows, is totally and miserably untrue.

Many explanations have been put forward as to why the Madonna lily reappears triumphantly every year in cottage gardens and peters out in the gardens of those whose home ranks as a house rather than as a cottage. It has been suggested (a) that cottagers habitually throw their pails of soap-suds over the lilies, (b) that the dust of passing traffic smothers the stems with purifying grit, (c) that the bulbs remain undisturbed year after year. Now I should be perfectly willing to throw soap-suds by the gallon over my lilies, and to collect trugs-full of grit for them from the lanes, and above all I should be willing and happy to leave them where they were for as many years as they saw fit. I ask no better. I can imagine nothing which would give me greater pleasure than to see a group of Lilium candidum increasing season after season, in the happy confidence that they would never be disturbed so long as I was in control of their fate. I would, in short, do anything to please them, but all my efforts have led me to the sad conclusion that the Madonna lily, like the wind, bloweth where it listeth.

There is a great deal more I could say on the subject of the Madonna lily, but I had started out with the intention of writing about Lilium auratum. Less wayward than candidum, in fact not wayward at all, there is no reason why the golden-rayed lily of Japan should not grow satisfactorily for all of us. It is said that the Japanese complacently eat the bulbs as a vegetable, much as we eat the potato or the artichoke, but fortunately for us they have also realised the commercial value to European gardens, and the slopes of Fujiyama yield a profitable harvest of bulbs which reaches this country shortly after New Year's Day. There are two ways in which we can grow this superb lily: in the open, preferably with the protection of shrubs, or in pots. I do not, myself, very much like the association of lilies with shrubs. It always looks to me too much like the-thing-one-has-been-told-is-the-right-thing-to-do. It savours too much of the detestable shrubbery border effect, and

suggests all too clearly that the lilies have been added in order to give 'an interest after the flowering shrubs are over'. This is not quite fair an accusation, since shrubs do certainly provide an ideal shelter for lilies, but still I retain a personal distaste for the arrangement. I cannot agree, for instance, that lilies look more 'handsome' against a background of rhododendron or azalea; I think they look infinitely more handsome standing independently in pots set, let us say, on a flight of garden steps. Of course this method involves a little more trouble. It means carrying the pots to the desired position, and watering them throughout the growing season. Still it is worth while, and if they can be placed somewhere near a garden bench their scent alone is sufficient justification.

Luckily, they are very amenable to life in pots, provided the pots are large enough and are filled with a rich enough compost of peat and leaf mould. It is as well to stake them when planting the bulbs, remembering that they may grow to a height of seven feet, especially the variety platyphyllum which is the finest of all. White and gold and curly, it unfolds to expose its leopard-like throat in truly superb and towering arrogance.

HEN THESE ESSAYS WERE WRITTEN BY VITA SACKVILLE-WEST in 1937, she probably never imagined that an American audience would be reading them. Much of our information about plants has changed since then, and of course American readers of *Some Flowers* should make the necessary adjustments with regard to discussion of climate, soil conditions, and proper planting seasons.

Many of the plants described in this book are available from nurseries in this country or by mail from specialty seed catalogues. Please note, however, the following: *Iris unguicularis*, *Primula pulverulenta*, and *Mutisia retusa* are less commonly found here; *Dianthus caesius*, *Primula littoniana*, and *Lilium giganteum* are now known by their correct names — *Dianthus gratianopolitanus*, *Primula vialii*, and *Cardiocrinum giganteum*. The illustrations of *Rosa*, *Centifolia Muscosa*, and *Rosa Gallica* were drawn from 'White Bath' and 'Tuscany Superb' respectively. Sources can be found in the triannual publication, *The Andersen Horticultural Libraries Source List of Plants and Seeds*, compiled by Richard Isaacson. This reference book is found in libraries, or may be ordered by mail from the publisher (The Andersen Library, Minnesota Landscape Arboretum, Box 39, Chanhassen, Minnesota 55317).